In Times *of*
TROUBLE

In Times *of* TROUBLE

Devotional Study for Women

KIMBERLIE A BLADES

XULON PRESS

Xulon Press
2301 Lucien Way #415
Maitland, FL 32751
407.339.4217
www.xulonpress.com

© 2023 by Kimberlie A Blades

All rights reserved solely by the author. The author guarantees all contents are original and do not infringe upon the legal rights of any other person or work. No part of this book may be reproduced in any form without the permission of the author.

Due to the changing nature of the Internet, if there are any web addresses, links, or URLs included in this manuscript, these may have been altered and may no longer be accessible. The views and opinions shared in this book belong solely to the author and do not necessarily reflect those of the publisher. The publisher therefore disclaims responsibility for the views or opinions expressed within the work.

Unless otherwise indicated, Scripture quotations taken from the New King James Version (NKJV). Copyright © 1982 by Thomas Nelson, Inc. Used by permission. All rights reserved.

Paperback ISBN-13: 978-1-66286-977-8
Ebook ISBN-13: 978-1-66286-978-5

Dedication

FROM THE TIME I was a little girl, I knew about God. It was told to me that Jesus was the only way to get through life. I often considered what it would be like to live a non-Christian life; however, that is not what God had in store for me. The older I got, the more I grew as a Christian. The majority of my family, on both my mom and dad's side, kept me in church no matter what, even when I was too tired or moody to go. My Grandma Angie was my biggest influence when it came to knowing who Jesus is. She would always make sure we were up and ready for church every Sunday and Wednesday; I'm telling you, we never missed a service unless we were running a fever! For Grandma to handle things so gracefully, it showed me that I could be that person too. I wanted to be a godly woman like her when I got older. If we acted up in church, she was so patient and never showed an attitude. I'm 100 percent sure that we made her mad a few times, but it never came across that way.

I look back on a time when she took me into her Sunday school class with her and my Papa Pat. I was always there looking in her Bible or reading her Sunday school paper. I felt like I was mature and I could handle the adult class because I was copying her actions and attitude. As time went on, Grandma Angie kept the same routine, not just with me but with all our family members as well. We would pray over every meal and in between. Even now that we are adults, she never goes without telling us how proud of us she is and how blessed she is by all of us. This kind and gentle attitude says a lot when we as grandchildren try to replicate those same characteristics in our everyday lives.

My mother, Bobbie Sue, is another major influence in my Christian walk. She and my dad kept my siblings and I in church as well. I remember going to an Apostolic church, where I was able to use my talent of dance for the Lord and not the world. This was the most exciting step in my longing for Christ. I knew that through dance, the chains on my life would be broken, and dance is where I received healing and deliverance. Oh man, did I cherish this talent. I felt as if I grew deeper in love with Christ and craved more and more of Him from that moment on.

Introduction:

GOD LAID IT on my heart to write this book years ago. Through life's challenges and hardships, the Lord said to me, "The time is now. Write My message." I thought to myself, *Wow, Lord, You are awesome!* I knew from the moment I woke up on this day that it was meant for me to finish what He (the Lord) had me start. I have a heart for hurting women, whether they have been hurt by men or other women. The Lord has called me to women's ministry, and I love it! I pray that as you are reading this and studying the Word that the Lord will open your eyes to what you have been blinded to.

Dear Heavenly Father,

I come to You right now and ask that whoever reads this will gain more understanding and knowledge of who they are in You and how they can become a strong woman of God. Lord, we come against all negativity right now in the mighty name of Jesus. Amen!

Table of Contents

Dedication v
Introduction: vii

Have you ever felt like you were alone in life?. 1
Have you ever tried to justify your actions? 4
What kinds of actions have you been taking t
   oward others lately?. 6
Am I beautiful enough to be loved? 8
How can we love those who try to bring us down? 11
Affirmation 14
Wisdom vs Knowledge: Fear of the Lord 16
When faced with fear, will you run, or will you
   stand and fight? 18
Are you right with God? 20
Being afraid of what others say: 23
Boiling my pressure:. 28
Active Faith: THE PATHWAY OF MIRACLES 32
Having the gift of faith 36

ENDURANCE... 39

Three truths about the words we speak 42

I am going to be completely transparent for just a moment. 46

Will work together for your good...................... 49

When affliction diminishes or enlarges you:............. 52

Affliction is part of life 55

Are you stuck in a bad relationship or situation
    in your life?... 59

How do you worship? 63

Attraction.. 65

Plug into your source of strength 68

His yoke is designed for you 70

Be still and know that I am God!...................... 73

Ask yourself this: If God loved us when we were
    helpless, ungodly enemies, how much more will
    He love us now that we are His children? 75

Ladies, have you ever been so disturbed by something
    or someone that you can't think straight?............ 78

Speaking and acting with wisdom and common sense 81

Have you ever felt like you were alone in life?

YOU HAVE FAMILY and friends, yet you still feel alone. I know I have felt this way on many occasions. I knew I had God on my side, but where was He? Was He really listening to me? Had I fallen so far away that He had let me go? These were questions that I struggled with for years, even though I went to church and prayed.

There was more to it, though. God really brought me to a point in my life where I had nothing and no one to turn to but Him. Physically, I had my children and family, but emotionally, I was lost. In my very soul, it felt like I was drowning in my circumstances and couldn't see anything but darkness.

There were times when I questioned God and the plan He had for me until one day, through it all, I woke up with the courage to take on the world. I had the courage to leave what had been a hinderance to me emotionally, physically, and spiritually. I never thought that I could do it and ignored what God was trying to tell me for years because I was focused on my circumstances instead of Him. So, I endured heartache and pain all at my own hands because I didn't see a way out.

Ultimately, God had a different plan for my life. I always prayed to Him, even in my darkest hour, and in all the moments

I questioned Him or where He was, He was listening and guiding my every move, every day, in every way. I praise God for where I am today and how far I have come.

- Reflect on a time in your life when you felt alone.

  _____
  _____
  _____
  _____
  _____
  _____

- When no one was around and you still made it through, do you believe it was God who brought you through the struggle?

  _____
  _____
  _____
  _____
  _____
  _____

- How did you feel once you noticed God was there?

  _____
  _____
  _____
  _____
  _____

When you pass through the waters, I will be with you; and when you pass through the rivers, they will not sweep over you. When you walk through the fire, you will not be burned; the flames will not set you ablaze.

Isaiah 43:2

Have you ever tried to justify your actions?

AS A YOUNG girl, I was told that "two wrongs do not make a right." I have carried this throughout my life. There were times when I felt like an awful person due to my actions and harsh words spoken to other people. We all try to justify our actions and never stop to think of the damage they cause.

All too often, when we do or say something hurtful to someone, we say, "Oh, I am just human, and God loves me for who I am." Boy, are we wrong! God made each of us in unique ways, yes, and He most definitely loves us, but that doesn't mean we are allowed to get away with revenge, being rude, saying bad things, and so forth.

If we really dig deep into the Word and get on our knees in prayer and ask God to reveal to us what needs to be changed, He will show us. He is not going to do it for us, but He will give us the strength to make the changes. Never think that doing to others what they do to you is right unless it's kind, loving, and caring. Instead, remember that we are to "do unto others as you would have them do to you."

Do to others as you would have them do to you.

Luke 6:31 KJV

Let this be a reminder that if we allow God to work through us, we will be able to make the changes to become a more loving, kind, and forgiving person that He calls us to be.

- When was the last time you chose to do something to someone because you thought it would feel good to get back at him/her? _____
- Did you feel convicted when you did the action? _____

- Did you try to make things right with that person? _____ Do not conform to the pattern of this world but be transformed by the renewing of your mind. Then you will be able to test and approve what God's will is—his good, pleasing, and perfect will.

Romans 12:2

What kinds of actions have you been taking toward others lately?

I OFTEN FIND myself, unintentionally, looking at someone with a wrong look. I sometimes want to scream at people when I feel they are being annoying or just don't know how to drive, etc. There are so many ways our actions can cause others to not see Christ in us. How can this change?

If we want to have the right actions, then we need to have godly motives.

All godly motives begin with the "renewing of the mind." Right thinking produces right actions. Our actions are the fruit of our deepest thoughts.

> In Us: Thinking and being like Christ are requirements not only for an individual but also for the corporate body of believers. Together we need to think and act like one being, like the Person of Jesus Christ.
>
> Philippians 2:1-5

Tip:

My husband tells me all the time that it's not what a person says that matters; it's what they are not saying and their actions behind their attitude.

So, listen carefully. Don't just cut people off. Really listen to what they don't say.

TO DO LIST:

- Say something kind and loving to another person.
- Be quick to listen and slow to speak.
- Replace anger with love.

Am I beautiful enough to be loved?

THERE COMES A time in life when all you can do is just give things to God and let go. You are beautiful! Not all people will agree with this statement because there is so much judgement out there that can really tear someone down mentally, spiritually, and physically.

We are not to listen to people who are negative toward us or others. What we should do is show love to those who show hate. They will eventually see what God is doing in your life, all because you were kind to them.

If you struggle with not being accepted, well, guess what? You are, and you are so loved and beautiful. God formed us. We are the clay, and He is still molding us so we can fulfill what He has called us to do. We must reach our destiny in life, and the only way to do so is by allowing Christ to come into our lives and walk the path He has chosen for us.

> Do not be anxious about anything, but in every situation, by prayer and petition, with thanksgiving, present your requests to God. And the peace of God, which transcends all understanding, will guard your hearts and your minds in Christ Jesus.
>
> Philippians 4:6-7

Beauty comes from within. It is not what we look like on the outside, although God does want us to take care of ourselves. Our bodies are a temple of the Holy Spirit, and we should treat them as such.

> Your beauty should not come from outward adornment, such as elaborate hairstyles and the wearing of gold jewelry or fine clothes. Rather, it should be that of your inner self, the unfading beauty of a gentle and quiet spirit, which is of great worth in God's sight.
>
> 1 Peter 3:3-4

+ When you wake up in the mornings, do you spend time with God before anything else?

_____

_____

_____

_____

+ If not, what can you do different so that the glory of God shines through you?

_____

_____

_____

_____

- Tip: Every morning, you should wake up and spend time with the Lord first and then prepare yourself for the day. My mother always told me that you never know who you will encounter that day. Always dress your best, even if it's jeans or shorts. Let Christ shine through your appearance.

How can we love those who try to bring us down?

I NEVER REALLY understood that loving those around you could be a hard thing to do. I was always taught to "love your enemies." I never thought that in my adulthood, I would have people who did not like me.

See, I was in a MVA (Motor Vehicle Accident) on March 1, 2005. I had all three of my children with me, all of whom were babies, little babies. Before I got into the accident, I had a verbal altercation with my mom and my older sister. I felt judged and like I didn't belong. There was so much rivalry and hate. Though I still loved them very much, I didn't feel the same in return and had said very, very harsh words and hateful things to both my sister and my mom. I spoke death over my life that day. I told my mom and sister that I should have never been born and that they will never see me again nor the kids. After this I left, we were on our way to my father and was hit head on by another vehicle. This left me in life support. My children turned out okay other than my middle daughter Harmonie's broken legs. From the moment I realized what happened I knew that God taught me a life lesson. There is power in the tongue. We either speak life or death, blessing's or curses. This was the moment my life had changed forever.

Over the years, we have come to a place where we've realized that love can conquer all things. Never leave someone's presence without showing the love of God in some way. Sometimes in life, our flesh wants to lash out at those who are against us or do wrong to us, but this is not God's way.

Always love, even when it is hard to love those who seem to not love or care for you in return; I know this feeling. Yet, I still stand strong on what I believe to be true, and that is loving unconditionally, and I try to do my best. We sometimes put conditions on our love toward others, but that is not what Christ wants from us. We are to love others as He loves us.

Matthew 5:43-44 says, "You have heard that it was said, You shall love your neighbor and hate your enemy. But I say to you, love your enemies, bless those who curse you, do good to those who hate you, and pray for those who spitefully use you and persecute you."

- Has there been some sort of trauma in your life that has put a separation between you and your loved ones?

_____

_____

_____

_____

- How did you mend that separation?

_____

_____

_____

_____

If things are not where they should be, how can you do better with showing the love of Christ?

_____
_____
_____
_____

Affirmation

ALL OF US women and even men need affirmation occasionally. I recently tried to lose weight. Not for anyone else, but for God and myself. Even though I may seem like I have all the confidence in the world and love myself inside and out, there are times when I don't feel so beautiful. I had looked at a photo of myself one day and thought, *Wow, Kimberlie, you could be so much better-looking.* This was Satan trying to work his way into my mind and plant self-doubt and insecurity.

A lot of this stems from a past relationship and past hurt. However, God never intended for His children to live with self-disgust and self-pity. I know the man I am living my life with loves me for who I am and tells me I'm so beautiful. He tells me this all the time, and I love it because at times when I feel less than, it lifts me out of that rut. I thought I had failed as a parent because my youngest daughter chose to live with her dad. Once again, this amazing man reminds me of how great of a person I am and how my children do love me even when they don't show it.

> For we are God's handiwork, created in Christ Jesus to do good works, which God prepared in advance for us to do.
>
> Ephesians 2:10

Having someone to provide affirmation to you is one of the best gifts you can receive. They may not know how you are feeling, yet they say one word, and it brings peace to your heart.

> You are altogether beautiful, my darling, beautiful in every way.
>
> Song of Solomon 4:7

- Tip: Always provide compliments; even the slightest hug can turn someone's world around. Be affirmative and know you are a great person who Christ loves.
- How can you show affirmation today to yourself and another person?

_____
_____
_____
_____

By living a Christ-like life, is your attitude toward yourself that of love and kindness?

_____
_____
_____
_____

Wisdom vs Knowledge: Fear of the Lord

IN ORDER TO have wisdom, you must have knowledge of God and submit to His will. To know something but not know God overturns the value of having knowledge. Remember that "joyful is the person who finds wisdom, the one who gains understanding" (Prov. 3:13).

To know, perceive, and receive are ways we gain wisdom.

Wisdom is the ability to take knowledge and use it in the best way.

Example: Most parents speak words of caution to their children. They have been there and done the same things, and they know the outcomes. So, in turn, parents impart words of wisdom to guide their kiddos down the right path. Even when the kids seem to think their way is the best way, at least you have imparted that bit of wisdom in them so they know right from wrong.

God does the same with us. Half the time, we ignore what He says and decide to do things our own way, which can lead to destruction. If only we would just be still and know that His way is the best way and that His timing is perfect among all.

The fear of the Lord is the beginning of knowledge, but fools despise wisdom and instruction.

Proverbs 1:7

- What does Proverbs 23:23 say?

  _____
  _____
  _____
  _____

- How can you apply this scripture to your life?

  _____
  _____
  _____
  _____

- How can you apply this scripture when speaking to others?

  _____
  _____
  _____
  _____

We must fear God! He gave us life and breath in our lungs.

When faced with fear, will you run, or will you stand and fight?

THERE HAVE BEEN many times in my life when I felt like the only thing to do was run from my problems. I felt that if I had faced them, I wouldn't see the next day. Even though I read the Word and prayed all the time, I felt lost and alone. I felt like God had abandoned me in the midst of my storms, and without Him, all I had left to do was run.

I had nothing left in me. I had tried to kill myself, and during this never-ending tunnel, God met me where I was at, and by His grace, I am still here. At that moment, I knew no matter how much running I had done or how much I wanted to just give up, He has never failed me, nor will He. God was with me through every step of my life. Through my darkness, I found light, and now I am living my best life, all because of Christ Jesus. I was brought up knowing that you cannot get through life without God. My family was right; you will continuously live in doubt, shame, sorrow, and so on if you don't put all your trust and faith in Christ.

Since the Garden of Eden, humankind has been facing spiritual warfare, and at the heart of this negative resistance is the presence of fear. It's important to know that we were originally created without this emotion, and it was only after Adam and Eve sinned that the spiritual, physical, and mental curses came upon the human race.

> The thief cometh not, but for to steal, and to kill, and to destroy, but I am come that they might have life, and that they might have it more abundantly
>
> John 10:10

We can forget everything and run, or we can face everything and fight the Enemy with the Word and slap Satan in the face with his little tactics.

Please respond on how God has seen you through your darkest time.

_____
_____
_____
_____
_____
_____
_____
_____
_____
_____
_____
_____
_____

Are you right with God?

IN 1 JOHN 2:1-2, the Word tells us how John's purpose for writing this book was to keep us from sinning, even though, realistically, we will all commit an act of sin of some sort. God's grace is sufficient in that He sent His Son, Jesus, so that we can be forgiven of our sins. This means that we as Christians should live in humility without judging others and boasting in ourselves.

These three lusts can lead to judging others because they don't live like you or do what you expect of them.

- Lust of the flesh, desire for sensual pleasures.
- Lust of the eyes refers to covetousness and materialism.
- Pride of life is being proud of one's position in the world or his/her life.

If we call ourselves Christians and don't act accordingly, we are not true followers of Christ. James 4 implies that the conflict within us is between our sinful desires for pleasure and the desire for God's will. The source of conflict among believers is often linked to material things. John warns believers of lusting after the things of this world.

> Our struggle is not against flesh and blood but against spiritual hosts of wickedness in the heavenly places.
>
> Ephesians 6:12

We must know who we are in Christ and live like Christians, loving our brothers and sisters in Christ. We cannot live for the world and call ourselves believers. If we are born again, then there should be change in our lives. Christians manifest their nature by practicing righteousness. We cannot say we are a Christian just because we go to church. We are to represent God through our actions and words to others.

In 1 John 3:15, the Word tells us that those who do not love their fellow Christians are not living in the light but instead are living in darkness. When we are born again, that should change our thought process, and we will show the love of Christ to those around us.

We are to base our walk with the Lord on the truth He has given us. Believers who know God's standards and desires for us but fail to put these truths into practice in their lives will also not mature in Christ.

These are questions we should be asking ourselves and reflecting on so that we know where we stand and what we believe the most. Quite a bit of the people in the world live to gain what the world has instead of what God wants for their lives.

- How do you know your walk with God is right and good?

  _____
  _____
  _____
  _____
  _____

- Do you live by the Word or the world?

  _____
  _____
  _____
  _____
  _____

- Do you desire the works of the flesh or what God has for your life?

  _____
  _____
  _____
  _____
  _____

Being afraid of what others say:

Happy is the man who finds wisdom, and the man who gains understanding.

> Proverbs 3:15

I OFTEN FIND myself living in fear of what others say or how they react to situations. It is difficult for me as a grown woman, wife, and mother to make decisions for what is best for my family because of such fear. I am learning day by day how to deal with what others say. It is a sin to fear. God didn't place us on this earth for us to live in fear but to have peace of mind.

My son, let them not depart from your eyes—

Keep sound wisdom and discretion; So, they will be life to your soul and grace to your neck. Then you will walk safely in your way, and your foot will not stumble. When you lie down, you will not be afraid; Yes, you will lie down, and your sleep will be sweet.

> Proverbs 3:21-24

People often say they don't care what others have to say about them, and that is great! Why can't it be that easy for all of us? If you start paying less attention to what makes you who you are—your talents, beliefs, and values—and start conforming to what others may or may not think, you'll harm your potential. You'll start playing it safe and tell people the truth in soft, easy ways instead of being bold because you're afraid of what will happen on the other side of the critique. You'll fear being ridiculed or rejected, and when challenged, you'll surrender your viewpoint. You won't raise your hand when you can't control the outcome and won't go for that promotion because you won't think you're qualified. You ultimately will live in fear, especially if it has to do with those closest to you.

> But even after that we had suffered before, and were shamefully entreated, as ye know, at Philippi, we were bold in our God to speak unto you (Gentiles) the gospel of God with much contention.
>
> 1 Thessalonians 2:2

As I was studying the Word of God last night, God opened my eyes to the way I should handle tough situations with confrontational individuals. He showed me that I don't have to live in fear, and I refuse to do so any longer. Fear caused my husband and I to lose something so precious and dear. See, I lacked something called *boldness*. I don't like dealing with confrontation and prefer for people to say what they need to without being rude and then walk away.

What used to stop me from being bold is that I wanted to be liked and seen as nice. I didn't want to have to deal with anyone being upset or offended by what I had said. It's worked for me in many ways, but it also held me back. Sometimes when I wanted to say something bold, I stayed silent because I just imagined a nameless disaster. But when I thought it through and asked myself, *What's the worst thing that could happen?* then I realized that the worst that will happen is that the person I'm speaking to might be upset for a day. Can I handle that? Yes, I can! And often, they don't even get upset for more than five minutes. They just thank me for being straightforward! Often, the consequences that we fear from being bold don't materialize.

Do not be afraid of sudden terror,

> Nor of trouble from the wicked when it comes; For the LORD will be your confidence and will keep your foot from being caught. Do not withhold good from those to whom it is due, when it is in the power of your hand to do so. Do not say to your neighbor Go, and come back, and tomorrow I will give it, when you have it with you. Do not devise evil against your neighbor, for he dwells by you for safety's sake. Do not strive with a man without cause, if he has done you no harm.
>
> Proverbs 3:25-30

This is God showing me what I need to do. I need to guard my heart and speak with boldness. I must stop letting others take advantage of me in ways that make me live in fear. "For we do not fight against flesh and blood, but against principalities, against powers, against the rulers of the darkness of this age, against spiritual hosts of wickedness in the heavenly places" (Eph. 6:12 NKJV). I must keep in my heart and in my mind that God is my confidence and no one can harm me spiritually, emotionally, or physically. It is time to stand up for myself and know that God fights my battles. All I must do is speak with *boldness*.

Remember that neighborly honesty is a practical application of wisdom and boldness is an outspokenness, unreserved utterance, freedom of speech with frankness, candor, cheerful courage, and the opposite of cowardice, timidity, or fear. Never let fear of what others may or may not say stop you from being honest and bold in the right way.

What do you think of when you hear the words "practical application of boldness"?

_____
_____
_____
_____
_____

How can you become bolder and more outspoken when it comes to ministering or witnessing to others?

_____
_____
_____
_____
_____

How do you feel about Proverbs 3:25-30?

_____
_____
_____
_____

Boiling my pressure:

MANY PEOPLE OFTEN find themselves having a hard time when it comes to letting things get to them, which can cause your "pressure to boil." My husband takes blood pressure medicine. I often tell him he is too extra when it comes to things. Not only him, but I also allow things to get to me at times. It is so simple for things to just bother him though, yet at the same time, he controls it very well.

How can we learn to live in peace and stay calm through things that normally would get on our nerves? Let's look at what the Word of God tells us.

> A soft answer turns away wrath,
> But a harsh word stirs up anger.
> The tongue of the wise uses knowledge rightly,
> But the mouth of fools pours forth foolishness.
>
> Proverbs 15:1-2

Pressure cooking was a common cooking method in many homes. Before microwaves, it was necessary to cook more on top of the stove. Pressure cookers are a handy way to cook both meat and vegetables more quickly while using less energy.

The liquid placed inside the pressure cooker with the contents releases steam inside the sealed container. A weight-operated valve placed on the top allows some steam and pressure to be released to avoid explosion. The dancing of the valve weight makes a sound as it allows steam to release. Great care must be taken in handling the pressure-filled container once the cooking is done. The built-up steam could hurt people or destroy the home as well as the long-awaited dinner if steps are not followed.

> Fools vent all their anger,
> But the wise quietly holds it back.
>
> Proverbs 29:11

This is the same when it comes to relationships with others or even just within yourself. It's as if we battle every day with not letting things get to us, especially when it comes to others.

> So then, my beloved brethren, let every man be swift to hear, slow to speak, slow to wrath; for the wrath of man does not produce the righteousness of God.
>
> James 1:19-20

If we do not release the boiling within our emotions to Jesus, an eruption of angry words may proceed. Unfortunately, harsh words can be forgiven but not taken back from being heard. To avoid damage in our relationships with family and close friends, we must be aware of the need to keep love in our hearts. We need Jesus's help to keep the extra pressure covered and contained until the heat can recede before reopening conversation on the difficult topic.

The same applies to if we were to talk badly about ourselves; then you're speaking harsh words against yourself that can be hard to reverse.

Here are some ways to hold your tongue in times of frustration:

1.) Ask the Holy Spirit for wisdom and to place gentle words within you.
2.) Take breaks to process an issue.
3.) Calmly discuss the issue and allow each person to release their thoughts shared in love.
4.) Set the issue aside for a while as both parties cool off, as if you were letting the pressure settle in a pressure cooker before opening the top.
5.) Be aware that those times when we're overly tired, stressed, or disappointed can also help us invite Jesus to love the other person through us.
6.) Always make peace prior to laying your head down at night.

Rest in Jesus, knowing He will release the pressure as you talk with Him and let Him know how you are feeling. I tell my husband all the time, "Babe, it's okay, everything will be fine." If it is something small, then why worry yourself with it? If it is something that can be cleaned up, then why bother with fussing? Life is full of mess-ups, but we don't have to let those mess-ups mess us up. I know how frustrating it can be when things go awry. I cannot stand procrastination or when someone gets frustrated over the little things, but it isn't for me to go crazy over and say ugly things because it boils my pressure. No, absolutely not!

We must give those little pet-peeves to God and ask Him to give us peace and let Him release our pressure. Once we can accomplish giving our all to Him, then and only then can we live in peace.

Active Faith: THE PATHWAY OF MIRACLES

> For as the body without the spirit is dead, so Faith without works is dead also.
>
> James 2:26

FAITH INEVITABLY CALLS us forward to action (to work within faith). After seeing the perfect will of God for our lives or ministry, and often after other doors remain closed, God opens unexpected doors intended to usher us into His destiny for our lives.

> I know your works. See I have set before you an open door, and no one can shut it; for you have a little strength, have kept My word, and have not denied my name.
>
> Revelation 3:8

When He open those doors for you and it's clearly no question that God's the one opening them, not you or anyone else, *move forward!* Such signs direct along His miraculous pathway and lead toward His realized will and purpose.

> So, David inquired of the LORD, saying, "Shall I go up against the Philistines? Will You deliver them into my hand?" And the LORD said to David, "Go up, for I will doubtless deliver the Philistines into your hand." So, David went to Baal Perazim, and David defeated them there; and he said, "The LORD has broken through my enemies before me, like a breakthrough of water." Therefore, he called the name of that place Baal Perazim. And they left their images there, and David and his men carried them away. Then the Philistines went up once again and deployed themselves in the Valley of Rephaim. Therefore, David inquired of the LORD, and He said, "You shall not go up; circle around behind them and come upon them in front of the mulberry trees. And it shall be, when you hear the sound of marching in the tops of the mulberry trees, then you shall advance quickly. For then the LORD will go out before you to strike the camp of the Philistines." And David did so, as the LORD commanded him; and he drove back the Philistines from Geba as far as Gezer.
>
> 2 Samuel 5:19-25

If we wait in His presence, eventually we'll be led to recognizing His moment. When God presents a clear, divinely given opportunity, act on it!

There is a practical harmony or synergism between vertical faith in God and horizontal works to a needy world. Faith is both spiritual and practical.

> Do you see that Faith was working together with his works, and by works Faith was made perfect…You see then that a man is justified by works, and not by Faith only.
>
> James 2:22, 24

> What does it profit, my brethren, if someone says he has Faith but does not have works? Can Faith save him?
>
> James 2:14

The question is literally, can that kind of faith (the kind that does not issue in good works) save him? The answer is no!

Remember that faith without works is dead, and vice versa. How do we expect God to use us if we don't exercise our faith along with good works? We would be a dead vessel and not usable.

The walk of faith is a glorious process of becoming increasingly free in Christ. By faith in Jesus's resurrection, we become free from the fear of death. Through faith in Jesus as our High Priest, we know that we have one who understands our temptations and can help us in remaining free from sin. By faith in Jesus's holiness in our lives, we are free to boldly enter God's presence without hesitation. Continue to put your faith in Jesus daily, and along with that, do good works.

- Faith without works is _____
- Has God opened a door for you to walk through and you wound up shutting it? _____
- Tip: Be mindful of the works of the Enemy and seducing spirits that can cause you to stumble and miss the door that God has for you.

Having the gift of faith

WHAT IS FAITH? Faith is having conviction, confidence, trust, belief, and reliance in something greater than anyone in this world. Walking in faith gives us the opportunity to trust God to fulfill His Word, to trust His character, and to believe what the Bible teaches. Following God is an exciting journey of faith!

> And those who know Your name will put their trust in You; For You, Lord, have not forsaken those who seek You.
>
> Psalm 9:10

Basically, if you trust in the Lord, then you can confidently believe that He will never leave you or abandon you.

Most people in the world find the idea of spiritual gifts confusing, scary, or weird. The Holy Spirit is not meant to scare us. He is God within us, and His gifts help us to build each other and the church up in supernatural ways.

God—because He is just amazingly awesome—has given each of us an opportunity to be part of bringing His kingdom to earth. When we are in sync with the Holy Spirit and humbly using the spiritual gifts He's given us, others get a glimpse of God's presence through us.

The idea that we have spiritual gifts, these are abilities that are not of this world, can be hard for our human minds to grasp. The Bible helps us understand what spiritual gifts are, why they exist, and how to use them every moment of every day.

I am very excited to say that I have the gift of faith. By putting full trust in the Lord, even when things don't seem to go the way I expect, God has never let me down. I know that by following His Word and giving my all to Him, having faith, believing, being confident, and having conviction, I am where I am today. I was brought from something horrible to a life full of happiness and laughter.

We are not always going to get the things we want, and that's okay. If you're going through something hard, your bills are coming due, your health is declining, etc., have faith and believe that God has something greater in the works.

> But the manifestation of the Spirit is given to each one for the profit of all: for to one is given the word of wisdom through the Spirit, to another the word of knowledge through the same Spirit, to another faith by the same Spirit, to another gifts of healings by [a]the same Spirit, to another the working of miracles, to another prophecy, to another discerning of spirits, to another different kinds of tongues, to another the interpretation of tongues. But one and the same Spirit works all these things, distributing to each one individually as He wills.
>
> 1 Corinthians 12:7-11 NKJV

Think of a time when your faith kicked in more so than any other time in your life. I encourage you to write about it, and when you are done, look at the miracle God did for you.

_____
_____
_____
_____
_____
_____
_____
_____
_____
_____
_____
_____
_____

ENDURANCE

FOR MANY OF us, the word "endurance" tends to bring to mind an elite athlete–the marathon runner, Ironman triathlete, or Olympian who has trained his or her whole life for a single shot at gold. But endurance in the game of life is something we all must learn.

Like faith, endurance is muscle. The more life asks us to endure, the stronger we grow. In learning to endure, we are accepting both timing we can't control and choosing to believe that the wait itself has purpose. And so, we wait for dreams to come true—a job, a spouse, a child—or for the intangible things in life—healing, peace, joy. We wait through seasons for one to end or another to begin.

Developing endurance is neither easy nor comfortable, but it is worth it. Learning to trust the Father's goodness even when the path before us is dim is what stimulates growth in our faith.

Sometimes God levels the mountain in our way. But in the moments when He doesn't, we can rest in the fact that His Holy Spirit has already given us everything we need to endure the climb over it. And when we do, we find ourselves changed, for God wastes nothing. And in endurance, we build character.
Thoughts & Questions for Journaling:

We are all enduring something.

- What has God already shown you about Himself while you wait?

  _____
  _____
  _____
  _____
  _____

- What has He shown you about yourself?

  _____
  _____
  _____
  _____
  _____

- How is waiting pushing you out of your comfort zone?

  _____
  _____
  _____
  _____
  _____

- What would it look like to rest in His goodness today, even though you may feel tired or discouraged?

_____
_____
_____
_____
_____

Prayer:

Father, this life can be hard to endure sometimes. But we know that in You, we have been given everything we need to overcome. Thank You for walking every road with us, guiding us each step of the way, and carrying us when we can't take another step on our own. We ask for Your strength and Your peace during the days that seem too hard to bear. Help us to put our faith in You regardless of our circumstances and to trust that nothing is too much for You.

And the Lord, He is the One who goes before you. He will be with you; He will not leave you nor forsake you; do not fear nor be dismayed.

Three truths about the words we speak

TO START CHANGING things for the better, we first need to recognize three essential truths about the nature of words. If we can begin to work these truths into our thinking, they will help us steer away from words that bring death and toward words that create life.

1. Words are a gift from God.

    - The ability to use words at all is a gift that has been given to all of us by our Creator. As such, we have a responsibility to use our words well. As we've seen, God was the first one to harness the creative force of words, and He has entrusted us with the same ability to use words to create the world around us. Given the substantial nature of this gift, we can't just throw our words around any old way we please; they contain too much power. The only acceptable response to the gift we've been given is to show respect to the Giver by using it well.

2. Words can build up or tear down.

    + As a kid, you probably chanted the phrase "Sticks and stones may break my bones, but words will never hurt me." I know I did. With a little age and experience, we come to realize that even though it sounds good in theory, the phrase is just plain wrong. Words can hurt. I bet you don't have any problem remembering the last harsh words that were spoken to you or the last encouraging words you received. Other people's words can have an incredible impact on us, whether we want them to or not. They have the ability to create the atmosphere of our lives. They also can create atmosphere for others.

3. The quality of your life is determined by the quality of your words.

    + The way you choose to communicate will ultimately affect every area of your life. Words aren't neutral. Every word that goes out has a consequence attached to it. How you speak to your friends, family members, and coworkers will determine the quality of those relationships. Your internal dialogue with yourself will determine the quality of your actions and interactions each day. It naturally follows that the quality of your life is determined by the words you speak.

Death and life are in the power of the tongue,
those who love it will eat its fruit.

> Proverbs 18:21

If we don't watch how we speak to others, then we can cause people to stumble, even if we don't intend to. Sometimes we feel the need to tell someone something, but is it what is supposed to be said in that moment, or do we just feel like being judgmental of that person?

- Do you often watch what you say or how you say things?

  _____
  _____
  _____
  _____
  _____

- How do you normally react if someone says something negative to you?

  _____
  _____
  _____
  _____
  _____

- How can you react better when someone comes at you sideways with words?

_____
_____
_____
_____
_____

I am going to be completely transparent for just a moment.

I ALWAYS THOUGHT marriage was a one-way street. I didn't believe there was a such thing as the "perfect marriage."

If God is at the center of your marriage, then in my personal opinion, that is a perfect marriage. I say that because if your relationship is a "God thing," then it's perfect for the two of you. If you feel you must hide who you are because of your spouse's reaction, then it's not a God thing; it is of fear.

Marriage is a union, a bond between man and woman. When God places you with His perfect match for you, then no one or nothing can tear you apart. Satan finds little sneaky doorways, however, to slip right through and cause turmoil, heartache, pain, fear, and overall bitterness toward one another.

Often, we just grow tired of always being the one to give. This is usually false thinking, but it still gets stuck in our brains anyway: *I'm always doing the dishes. She never takes out the trash. I always have to take care of the baby.* In reality, we aren't the only ones who do all those things.

True love is work. In a perfect world, the feelings of love could carry us through any difficult day or hard time, but the feelings don't last forever. The work lasts forever: even when our independent natures don't want to do the work or put in the effort at times.

We have been led to believe that marriage shouldn't be this much work; however, it really takes effort to build a new life together. It doesn't matter if you are bringing a past experience into a new relationship or if you are building from square one for the first time; true love requires diligent attention to removing selfishness from the equation.

Practice putting down the game controller, the laptop, or the cellphone and give your spouse the attention he/she deserves when they are talking. Let him/her know they are more important than the other things you have going on. True love calls us to treat each other with humility and gentleness. Father, lead us into gentleness and humility as we learn to love each other well. Thank You for enabling us to do this work together.

These questions may get pretty personal; however, for healing purposes, you need to answer these questions. I thought I had gotten over what happened in my past relationship. It took a lot of prayer and counseling before I knew I had to forgive myself first.

- Have you ever been in a marriage that was a total disaster?

_____
_____
_____
_____
_____

- Were you able to escape the marriage?

  _____
  _____
  _____
  _____
  _____

- Did you feel convicted over leaving the marriage?

  _____
  _____
  _____
  _____
  _____

- Did you replace that marriage with Christ or try to find something better right away?

  _____
  _____
  _____
  _____
  _____

Will work together for your good

> And we know that all things work together for good to them that love God, to them who are the called according to his purpose.
>
> Romans 8:28

MANY PEOPLE HEAR this verse and question, "What good can come out of this situation I'm going through, Lord?" I know because I asked the same thing.

Paul contrasts a life lived in selfish pursuits (the flesh) and one lived in league with, or in accordance with, God (the Spirit). He impresses upon readers that our sovereign God is all-knowing, all-wise, and all-powerful.

We can get so caught up in our circumstances or problems that we fail to look at what God wants from us during them. We can often fail at seeking God and instead get ourselves worked up over something that He has the ultimate control over. We need to remind ourselves that God does work *all* things together for good. As God is glorified, His people get to benefit the rewards.

The promise that God works all things together for good does not mean that all things, taken by themselves, are good.

Some things and events are decidedly bad. But God is able to work them together for good. He sees the big picture; He has a master plan. It is up to us to put our complete trust in Him and know the plans He has for us.

> "For I know the plans I have for you," declares the Lord, "plans to prosper you and not to harm you, plans to give you a hope and a future."
>
> Jeremiah 29:11

We need to hold on to His Word, seek Him constantly, and do what He tells or shows us to do. Push forward; don't look backward. If you look away from the path He has laid in front of you, then you will stumble and fall.

- How many times have you gotten caught up in the thought of "What good is this?"

_____

_____

_____

_____

- Have you stopped to tell yourself that "All things *will* work out if I just let God handle it"?

_____

_____

_____

_____

- Most of all, have you actually sought out God about the situation?

    _____
    _____
    _____
    _____

When affliction diminishes or enlarges you:

WHEN A CHILD learns to walk, he or she falls several times but gets up again until he or she succeeds. The child does not have a false identity. In contrast, when we grow up and fall, we usually stay on the floor.

The apostle Paul showed a good attitude in the face of adversity. He was in prison, not for committing a crime but for obeying his divine calling. He wrote a letter to the Philippians, where he said, "Rejoice in the Lord always, and again I will say rejoice!" (Phil. 4:4 NKJV). In the midst of whatever situation we are going through, we should understand that we are not to depend on circumstances but on the Spirit that has been given to us. We should be able to say, "In the midst of my condition, I rejoice in the Lord."

Paul was talking about his experiences in life. His secret is in Philippians 4:11–13. He says that he may be going through a difficult situation or be in abundance, but he remains the same. People often change through the extremes they live in. One extreme is positive, which is living in abundance. The other extreme is when we lack or are in need. However, both extremes reveal who we are through our reactions. Paul says,

"In Christ, I remain the same." Nothing changes us because we can do everything in Christ, who is the reason of our strength.

Paul proved to be a true apostle by demonstrating his resilience through his letters. He never presented his accomplishments, instead only presenting the facts. Through every hardship he experienced, he remained true to his calling. This is the greatest evidence of someone who possesses the life of the true God: that regardless of adversity, he or she continues to serve Him. Actions speak louder than words.

Paul said that he cared for and was burdened for the church. It was the suffering of others that weighed him down, not his own condition. This process in his life not only produced his knowledge of the God of all comfort but transformed him into an instrument of consolation for others. It makes sense because now he understood that why he suffered and what had happened in his life was God's preparation to enable him to comfort others.

I suffered through a lot of pain and hurt, physically and mentally. In the midst of moving from shelter to shelter with my kids, prior to my life now, I never let go of the One Who was there to see me through it all. The Lord allowed me to endure what I went through so it can give hope to others. It comforts me to know I can show God's light through my overcoming of torment.

Write a little bit about your past hurts in a relationship that you overcame.

_____

_____

_____

_____
_____
_____
_____
_____
_____
_____
_____
_____

It takes a lot to speak up when you have been hurt. It takes a lot for you to look up when you've been looked down on for so long, to smile when all you have done is cry, to love others after never receiving it in return, to trust others when you have lost all trust. But there is One who speaks for you, looks out for you, cries with you and smiles with you, One who loves you unconditionally and restores trust.

Overall, the One I'm speaking of is God. He formed you, and He knows everything you have been through and what your future holds. He knows and sees all. He loves each one of us, and He waits for us to seek Him both in times of trouble and in good times.

Jesus loves you. He will never leave you nor forsake you.

Affliction is part of life

Do not be anxious about anything, but in every situation, by prayer and petition, with thanksgiving, present your requests to God.

Philippians 4:6

PAUL SPEAKS ABOUT the human condition and what we go through in everyday life. This is important because although we do need to know the richness in the life of Christ, we should also know how to use it in adverse situations.

In the Book of Philippians, Paul teaches about the concerns we live through and the distress of the soul. We need to understand that afflictions are part of life. We cannot avoid them. Our life is not about living in these situations, but they are part of it.

Remember always that Jesus Himself told His disciples, "These things I have spoken to you, that in Me you may have peace. In the world you [a]will have tribulation; but be of good cheer, I have overcome the world" (John 16:33 NKJV). The followers of Jesus went through times of persecution. As children of God, we are not exempt from afflictions or trials. We have a victorious life; however, this does not mean we will avoid difficult times.

Paul does not deny that affliction exists or comes into our lives. Instead, he says to not be anxious about anything. Worry leads to bigger problems, such as anxiety and fear. When fear is in your heart and mind, it produces a state of anxiety that wraps you in a constant state of affliction. This is why Paul says to be anxious for absolutely nothing.

We have all been through worrisome situations. Personally, I have gone through things that caused a lot of fear and anxiety. We will continue to go through moments of distress that can produce anxiousness. But we must not convert difficult times into worry. Let's face it, worrying is a sin. When you worry, your concerns occupy your thoughts, and your heart is filled with fear. Instead, you must shift your thoughts into seeking God and get into the Word before the problem takes you to a crisis. The problem is that we tend to do this at the end of our difficult situation. Generally, people search for solutions any way they can, but before doing that, we need to go to God.

Here are some scriptures that will help you through difficult times.

- "It is the Lord who goes before you. He will be with you; he will not leave you or forsake you. Do not fear or be dismayed."—Deuteronomy 31:8
- "Even though I walk through the valley of the shadow of death, I will fear no evil, for you are with me; your rod and your staff, they comfort me."—Psalm 23:4

- "He sets on high those who are lowly, and those who mourn are lifted to safety."—Job 5:11
- "The steadfast love of the Lord never ceases; his mercies never come to an end; they are new every morning; great is your faithfulness."—Lamentations 3:22-23
- "Peace I leave with you; my peace I give to you. Not as the world gives do I give to you. Let not your hearts be troubled, neither let them be afraid."—John 14:27
- "God is our refuge and strength, a very present help in trouble."—Psalm 46:1
- "Blessed be the God and Father of our Lord Jesus Christ, the Father of mercies and God of all comfort."—2 Corinthians 1:3
- "Let your steadfast love comfort me according to your promise to your servant."—Psalm 119:76
- "I have said these things to you, that in me you may have peace. In the world you will have tribulation. But take heart; I have overcome the world."—John 16:33

What is the scripture that sticks out to you the most?

_____
_____
_____
_____
_____
_____
_____
_____

How can you apply this every morning during your time with God and throughout your day?

_____
_____
_____
_____
_____
_____
_____

Are you stuck in a bad relationship or situation in your life?

(I am going to open up a bit about myself.)

I KNOW THAT I sure have. I found myself in both a bad situation and a horrible relationship. See, for many years—seventeen to be exact—I was going through torment and physical pain. I was sexually abused quite a bit, mentally and emotionally abused, and physically beaten and abused. Life for me was not what I had thought it was going to be. My children and I jumped from shelter to shelter and from home to home to run from the very thing I had to face.

I knew that God was with me every step of the way, even when He opened a door for me and I seemed to slam it shut. I was always told it was the right thing to do to stay in the relationship, and people told me how much this person loved me, yet I knew different.

Every day I prayed, kept reading the Word, and thought I was doing what was right. I still felt isolated and alone, not physically but mentally, so much to the point that I ran my car off the road and God shut my engine down before I hit a tree head on. I didn't feel I could trust anyone, nor did I feel I had anyone on my side.

It wasn't until January of 2020 that I finally leaped through the door God had opened for me and pressed forward, no matter the consequences. I had to get to a place where I fully, 100 percent completely, relied on God. Now I have a life that I thought was only a fairytale.

God wants to comfort you and give you wisdom in times of darkness or confusion. Through a relationship with Him, we have a place to turn when we have nowhere else to go. If you feel hopeless or lost, you can find rest and comfort in the love of God today. Know that you're not alone. There is a God who loves you, who thought of you before you were born. He knows every hair on your head and formed you. Let Him have His way with you and direct your steps. You too can have a life full of peace and comfort. If you are suffering abuse or are hurting, reach out.

National Domestic Violence Hotline

800-799-7233

Text: Text START to 88788

Daily Prayer!

Dear Heavenly Father,

Forgive me of all my sins, I repent of all wrongdoing right now in the name of Jesus. Lord, I thank and praise You for who You have placed in my life. Thank You for my family and the calling You have placed on me. Without You in my life, I would have never made it to where I am today. Father God, thank You for never leaving nor forsaking me. I cannot make it without You. This is the day that You have made, and I shall rejoice in it. The joy of the Lord is my strength. I will rejoice and be glad in it! The joy that I have is not from the world. I received it because of You, and the world can't take that from me. I am so glad that You, Lord, are my Guide.

In Jesus's name, Amen.

I encourage you to write your own prayer that is between you and our Heavenly Father. Be intimate and real. He knows what is in your heart; bring it forth to Him. Seek His face. Ask and you shall receive.

How do you worship?

"If you're not worshiping God on Monday the way you did the day before, perhaps you're not worshiping him at all."

– A.W. Tozer

THIS QUOTE HAD me self-reflecting on if I worship Christ throughout the week like I do on Sundays. I know that I have a heart of worship. Worshiping God is an everyday thing. Worshiping the God in spirit and in truth is the genuine heart that anyone who seeks Him will have.

Let's look at John 4:20-24:

> Our fathers worshipped in this mountain; and you say, that in Jerusalem is the place where one ought to worship.
>
> Jesus said unto her, Woman, believe me, the hour comes, when you shall neither in this mountain, nor yet at Jerusalem, worship the Father.

You worship you know not what: we know what we worship: for salvation is of the Jews.

But the hour comes, and now is, when the true worshippers shall worship the Father in spirit and in truth: for the Father seeks such to worship Him.

God is Spirit: and they that worship Him must worship Him in spirit and in truth.

If on a Sunday, you are leading others into the presence of God, then you must praise and worship Him throughout the week as well. Your heart has to be in the right place. You cannot expect to be in His presence or to lead others if your heart is not in the right place. If you have a disrespectful attitude, don't think for one instant that God doesn't know your heart.

Your heart not being in the right place when it comes to serving God is unacceptable. Going through the motions without fearing God is like worshipping in vain.

- Are you really God's child, or are you just trying to get your fire insurance papers? We need to understand that we can't just say we are Christians and still live the worldly way. You either want to worship God fully and whole heartedly or you don't its your choice.

_____
_____
_____
_____

Attraction

Do not love the world or the things in the world. If anyone loves the world, the love of the Father is not in him. For all that is in the world—the desires of the flesh and the desires of the eyes and pride in possessions—is not from the Father but is from the world. And the world is passing away along with its desires, but whoever does the will of God abides forever.

1 John 2:15-17 ESV

Merciful God,

You have given humankind free will to think about whatsoever. However, that does not mean You are pleased with our thoughts. There are times when our thoughts may wander in every direction and veer off that which is in accordance with Your commandments and Your Word. Our thoughts reflect what's in our hearts.

IN LIFE TODAY, there is a hunger and thirst for people, things, objects, positions, power, titles, prestige, honor, recognition, wealth, and so much more. The primary desire, focus, ambition, and objective of the world are on things that are not eternal. This is not of You, Father God. I lift up everyone whose compulsive preoccupation with something or someone is consuming their lives. Lord, if there is obsession in our lives, let it be loving and doing what is right because it is of You. Our ambition should be in loving You and obeying Your will.

Bring forth the strength You have given us to face each day so we can be of service to others. God, we lay ourselves aside right now in the name of Jesus so we can be the disciples You have called us to be. In Jesus's mighty name, Amen.

> Finally, brothers and sisters, whatever is true, whatever is noble, whatever is right, whatever is pure, whatever is lovely, whatever is admirable—if anything is excellent or praiseworthy—think about such things.
>
> Philippians 4:8

- Where has your mind been lately?

_____
_____
_____
_____
_____
_____

- Are your thoughts in accordance with the Word of God?

  _____
  _____
  _____
  _____
  _____
  _____

Plug into your source of strength

AS WOMEN, OUR energizers often run dangerously low. We may try to plug into superficial power, such as an extra shot of coffee during the day or some sort of shopping. Perhaps we rely on our friends to give us that boost to make us feel important and needed, or we look to our spouse/boyfriend to fill our deep desire for love and affirmation.

But these power sources don't cut it. They can't quite get our battery to a full charge. We're left feeling agitated, lonely, run down, let down, and even defeated.

There is only one real energy source, and it is not found at the coffee pot. It is found in that moment when we come before the One Who understands every minute detail about us and longs to give power to those who know they are weary and weak before Him. We need to come to Him daily, not just when things are getting tough. This requires morning devotion, worship, and prayer. This means really digging deep into His Word and gaining knowledge of what it is that He wants us to do.

You may feel like you need a nap, but He never grows weary. You may feel weak in the knees as you struggle to understand how to handle a difficult relationship, but He gives you strength. He provides guidance and wisdom and fills every single need of your heart. His charge will take hold and fill you. But here's the catch: you need to plug into Him.

Maybe that means adding time with God to your calendar every morning or joining a Bible study to read Scripture in a fresh way. Maybe it means listening to a sermon podcast while you make dinner or reaching out to a friend as an accountability partner who will remind you of the only true source of strength—God Himself.

Whatever method you try, it will make a dramatic difference in your life. God may not remove the circumstances that fill up your day, but He will give you the strength to walk with Him through it. Connect with God.

Psalm 143:8—

> *"Cause me to hear thy lovingkindness in the morning; for in thee do I trust: cause me to know the way wherein I should walk; for I lift up my soul unto thee."*

His yoke is designed for you

I AM A mom of three beautiful children. As they were growing up, our funds ran low, so most of the times, their clothes came from hand-me-downs or the thrift store. I had no shame if it was just me, but when my kids were with me, I would feel embarrassed, especially if they felt embarrassed. I never thought about everyone being built differently. These clothes were definitely not custom fit to their bodies. Although the clothes they were given didn't fully fit, they covered them.

God is not like that. When Jesus says that a keyway to find rest is to "Take my yoke upon you," (Matthew 11:29 NKJV). He is gently rebuking us for taking on burdens that we were not meant to carry and telling us to instead take on those purposes that He has created just for us.

> Come to Me, all *you* who labor and are heavy laden, and I will give you rest. Take My yoke upon you and learn from Me, for I am [E]gentle and lowly in heart, and you will find rest for your souls. For My yoke *is* easy and My burden is light.
>
> Matthew 11:29

A yoke is a wooden beam normally used between a pair of oxen or other animals to enable them to pull together on a load when working in pairs, as oxen usually do; some yokes are fitted to individual animals. There are several types of yokes used in different cultures and for different types of oxen. Imagine how difficult it would be if one animal were to take on the yoke that was made for another. Each animal carries different weight loads, and if the wrong yoke is too big, then the animal carrying that yoke will be in pain and strain to get the job done.

Many times, we seem to carry loads or burdens that we were not meant to. The Lord says to cast our cares upon Him.

> So, humble yourselves under the mighty power of God, and at the right time he will lift you up in honor. Give all your worries and cares to God, for He cares about you.
>
> 1 Peter 5:6-7

+ List what cares or burdens you may have and hand them over to God.

_____
_____
_____
_____
_____

- How do you feel after you're done seeking the Father?

    _____
    _____
    _____
    _____
    _____

- Do you want that ultimate inner peace that comes with following Christ?

    _____
    _____
    _____
    _____
    _____

When I sit in the presence of the Lord our God. I'm in awe of how awesome He is. He is the Alpha and Omega; He's the beginning and the end. He is the God who knew us before we were formed in our mother's womb and knows our end before we even begin.

He knows the struggles and obstacles we will face in life, and because we are His children, He will work all things together for our good and for His glory. No matter what life throws at us, remember this—God is with you and is working it all out.

~Leroy Blades, Apostle

Be still and know that I am God!

Be still and know that I *am* God; I will be exalted among the nations, I will be exalted in the earth!

Psalm 46:10

MY HUSBAND AND I were in a situation where we had chosen to stay with our son at his place to help him out financially. At the time, it was just supposed to be Kaden (our son) and us in the house. We did not mind helping him, especially when it came to getting to and from work, and we chose to help with his bills and rent so he could save for a vehicle. However, he made a decision that put us in a position that was very difficult to get out of. My husband and I tried to find a place apart from our son to rent and searched our hearts out, but everything was too far away from where God had called us to be. I struggled with wanting to mother him again and tell him what to do and how to do it, and it started causing issues within my peace.

I knew we were to be elsewhere; however, God was telling us to be still. A dear friend of mine and I were speaking, and she said, "In every situation, we should never be too anxious to jump into something. We must go into any situation knowing that God has this. However, we also have to deal with our flesh. That's when the Holy Ghost comes in and we should apply the Word of God to every situation ... We always, always, always need to not try to handle the situation, whether large or small, without God."

I am a solutionist; I must find a solution for everything, even if it isn't a problem but needs an outcome. I struggle with this every day. The Lord has been dealing with me about not "putting the cart before the horse." My husband tells me this all the time. The question is, how do I learn to be still? How do I not try to find a solution to everything? It feels nearly impossible.

I tell myself that I don't need to try to fix everything, that God says in Psalm 46:10, "Be still and know that I am God, I will be exalted among the nations, I will be exalted in the earth." Throughout my life and its struggles, I have always felt like I have to have control. Even though I knew God was there to see me through every single situation, I struggled to let go of this mindset. But with knowledge comes change.

- What tough situation have you found yourself in that you just could not let go of trying to find a solution to?

_____
_____
_____
_____
_____
_____

Ask yourself this: If God loved us when we were helpless, ungodly enemies, how much more will He love us now that we are His children?

> But God demonstrates His own love toward us, in that while we were still sinners, Christ died for us. Much more then, having now been justified by His blood, we shall be saved from wrath through Him. For if we were enemies we were reconciled to God through the death of His Son, much more having been reconciled, we shall be saved by His life. And not only that, but we also rejoice in God through our Lord Jesus Christ, through whom we have now received the reconciliation.
>
> Romans 5:8-11

THROUGH THE BLOOD of Christ, believers are no longer enemies of God, and we no longer have to live in bondage. He loves us that much! To die on a cross for our sins was the ultimate sacrifice.

I tell my children that if it came between them and God, I would choose God because He chose me. Without Christ thinking of me, I wouldn't be here. This amazing God I serve loved me so much that He thought of me not only to have life but to be a parent myself. Wow! He gave me the greatest gift, and that is the heart to serve Him in all ways.

Lord,

I love You and praise You for all You have blessed me with. From the time You thought of me to where You have brought me today, I owe my life to You. I shout with joy and excitement knowing I have my Father on my side. In Jesus's name, Amen.

Write your own personal prayer:

_____
_____
_____
_____
_____
_____
_____
_____
_____
_____
_____
_____
_____

How much do you think God loves you?

_____
_____
_____
_____
_____
_____
_____
_____

Ladies, have you ever been so disturbed by something or someone that you can't think straight?

I KNOW THAT exact feeling. I have been struggling with a certain situation, and yet, I can't do anything about it. I want so much to just say words to this person, but God is giving me strength to hold my tongue. A lot stems from my past hurts and traumas.

We may not realize it at the time, but we often allow Satan to plant little seeds to bring up our pasts. Just when I believe I am delivered from this feeling of "Something's wrong; am I enough? Why is he/she talking to my spouse?" etc., Satan sneaks that doubt right back in. We must stop him in his tracks and say, "No! Get thee behind me, Satan!"

When I want to just go off, I just simply and calmly say, "Okay, God, You've got this. Lord, please take this feeling from me in the name of Jesus. You are my healer, my deliverer, my strength when I am weak, my fortress, and my shield from all unrighteousness."

How do we walk this life in peace if Satan is on our heels? Our minds are part of us, and for us to be healed, our minds also need healing and renewing. The Devil will try to come against God's people. There will be times when Satan will try to influence your thoughts and use them to stop or slow down your healing process.

> And they overcame him by the blood of the Lamb and by the word of their testimony, and they did not love their lives to the death.
>
> Revelation 12:11

This is the heavenly defeat of Satan.

We have great reason to rejoice during our healing journey. We have the one person who truly loves us no matter what we do or how we may act. We may go through things in life and things may rear back at us, but if we stay true to God's Word, stay in constant prayer, love unconditionally, and forgive even when it is hard to, then we can live a joyful and peaceful life that God has given us.

- If you are married or in a relationship, do you find yourself getting jealous at times?

  _____
  _____

- Ask yourself, is it because of the person or because of underlying past hurts and traumas?

  _____
  _____

- How can you turn that jealousy into an agape love?

_____
_____
_____
_____
_____
_____
_____

Speaking and acting with wisdom and common sense

I NOTICED AT times that I feel like I have a lack of common sense, yet at the same time, I also feel that I speak with wisdom. How can this be? The answer is that it can't. Common sense and wisdom go hand in hand. If we follow Christ and listen to God's direction, then we will make wise decisions. This is both common sense and wisdom put together. When we do this, then it leads to honor, prosperity, pleasantness, and peace.

Common sense: You won't get into debt if you don't spend more money than you make. The Holy Spirit doesn't need to speak audibly to tell us that we can't have more money going out than we have coming in. Common sense tells us that we'll get in trouble if we do that.

Wisdom: Wisdom teaches that you won't keep friends if you try to control and dominate everything that goes on in your life and theirs. You also won't keep friends if you talk about them behind their backs. Wisdom always leads to God's best for you and your life.

Wisdom and common sense are closely linked. Wisdom discerns truth in a situation, while common sense provides good judgment regarding what to do about the truth. Wisdom is supernatural—it isn't taught by men but is a gift from

God. Wisdom is our friend. It helps us to make choices now that we will be happy with later so we will not live in regret. Himosmnfks

- Do you feel as though you speak wisdom?

  _____

- How would you rate your common-sense level?

  _____

- Do you believe that both wisdom and common sense can be thought about as one?

  _____

As we go through life, we may find ourselves battling situations or things the Enemy (Satan) throws at us. In times like these, we should let God do the battling. There are times now that I find myself having to remember that God has everything in control as long as I allow Him to.

The Enemy will find every weak spot we have to work his little squirmy way in, but we have to recognize it and remind ourselves we are the head and not the tail; we are above and not beneath. When we speak the Word of God over our lives and our circumstances, then the Enemy has no choice but to flee. In Jesus's name.

I tell my kids all the time that living for Jesus Christ is the only way through this messy world. It is the only way to truly have peace and understanding. We may fall at times, and that is completely okay, but what is not okay is to stay down; it is not okay to allow the Enemy to have his way. So many times, Satan has tried to stop me from moving forward in my walk with God. He has tried to take my life on several occasions, but you know something. I did not let him win. I refused, and still continue to refuse, to allow him to have a foot hold in any part of my life. I allowed God to have His way in my life, and it has been the best decision I have ever made.

I encourage you to allow God to have His way. Allow Him to come into your life and show you what true peace is. I know what torment, heartache, loss, trauma, and mental and emotional abuse is, and I know what it can do to a person. However, you do not have to let it determine who you become.

You know, a lot of people ask the question, "Why do bad things happen to good people?" We may need to dissect this question for a moment. See, it is not that bad things happen to good people; it's that we live in a world filled with sin, and because of that sin, bad things happen to people. But thanks be to God that during those bad times, He makes the way for us to deal with it, building us up to walk in our calling so we can help others through the same or similar things. Any way you look at it, God works ALL things for our good and His glory. I know this from personal experience of things I have been through and how God has taught me. You may wonder if I regret what I have gone through, but the truth is, I don't. I know that I am now using what God allowed me to endure to help other women. Do I have unforgiveness toward the other people who hurt me? No, absolutely not, because it was Satan using him/her to bring me down. Trust me when I say, it has taken me some time to get to where I am now. It did not happen overnight but having God by my side is what truly helped me through it all. The Devil will try and complicate your healing process and put doubts in your mind; as I said before though, you have to recognize his schemes and put him in his place. He told me how worthless I was and how there was no one better for me in this life. Boy was he wrong.

See, life is strange. Every day, I am learning new things and learning new ways to better my personal walk with the Lord. I am a first-grade teacher, but most importantly, I am a pastor who loves the Lord with all her heart and still struggles at times—especially with the mom part! I know that God works with imperfections. By the grace of God, I am clothed with dignity and draped in His perfect love, as you are also.

Remember who you are in Christ. Remember how loved you are by our Lord. Remember how amazing you are and how special you are, not only to God but to those around you. I love you, and I am here for you. No woman or young lady should ever feel alone in this world.

www.ingramcontent.com/pod-product-compliance
Ingram Content Group UK Ltd.
Pitfield, Milton Keynes, MK11 3LW, UK
UKHW041946230426
12048UKWH00008B/161